BROWNIE
Cook Book

Compiled and edited by
MYRA STREET

Illustrated by
DEREK MATTHEWS

Hodder & Stoughton

MEMBER OF THE HODDER HEADLINE GROUP

Acknowledgements
The Editor and Publishers would like to thank the following for all their help with material and pictures.

Van den Berghs & Jurgens (Stork Cookery Service)
page	33	Face biscuits
	34-35	Marble cake and Dougal cake
	11	Pizzas

The British Egg Information Service
	7	Bacon and egg pitta
	18	Eggy toast, bacon and fried eggs
	19	Scrambled eggs, poached eggs
	20	Omelette/Oven potato and cheese pie

British Meat Information Service
	8	Croque-Monsieur
	13	Easy-mix scone pizza
	14	Beefy burgers
	15	Monster burgers
	16-17	Yankee beans and bangers
	22	Meat balls with pasta
	29	Porky baked potatoes

British Chicken Information Service
	25	Spicy dips with chicken strips
	26	Peanut chicken pasties
	27	Chicken nuggets with orangey peanut dip
	27	Barbecued sweet and sour drumsticks

Tate & Lyle Sugars
| | 39 | Toffee apples |
| | 41 | Fudge, Treacle toffee |

Summer Orange Office
	6	Sandwiches
	44	Jelly orange baskets
	45	Jelly slices/Orange animal biscuits

The Banana Group
	9	Banana croissants
	46	Frothy banana yoghurt
	46	Banana strawberry shake

Ocean Spray Cranberries
| | 47 | Sparkling cranberry cream |
| | | Cranberry party punch |

Silver Spoon – British Sugar Corporation plc
| | 36-37 | Meringue caterpillar |
| | 32 | Gingerbread men |

The Fresh Fruit and Vegetable Information Bureau
	23	Tomato pasta salad
	30	Sunshine salad
	31	Salami and potato salad

Flour Advisory Bureau
| | 12 | Quick crusty pizza |
| | 48 | Food Pyramid – Choosing a balanced diet |

British Library Cataloguing in Publication Data
Street, Myra
Brownie Cook Book
I. Title
641.5

ISBN 0—340—59831—X

First published 1993
Impression number 10 9 8 7 6 5 4 3 2 1
Year   1998 1997 1996 1995 1994 1993

Printed in Hong Kong for Hodder & Stoughton Educational — a division of Hodder Headline PLC, Mill Road, Dunton Green, Sevenoaks, Kent TN13 2YA by Colorcraft Ltd.
Produced with the full co-operation of the Girl Guides Association.

Complied and Edited—Myra Street
Design—Glynn Pickerill
Illustrations—Derek Matthews
Design Production—The R & B Partnership
Jacket—Hodder & Stoughton
For the Girl Guides Association—Vronwyn Thompson

Handy Measures
25g/1oz flour	= 3 level tablespoons
25g/1oz sugar	= 2 level tablespoons
25g/1oz butter	= 2 level tablespoons
25g/1oz grated cheese	= 4 level tablespoons
3 teaspoons	= 1 tablespoon

TEMPERATURES
°C	°F	Gas Mark	
130	250	1/2	Very Cool
140	275	1	Very Cool
150	300	2	Cool
160/170	325	3	Warm
180	350	4	Moderate
190	375	5	Fairly Hot
200	400	6	Fairly Hot
210/220	425	7	Hot
230	450	8	Very Hot
240	475	9	Very Hot

Contents

HAVE FUN Cooking

YOU WILL be amazed at how easy and satisfying it is to make simple dishes. There are certain dangers such as heat, gas, electricity and sharp knives involved when cooking. IT IS ESSENTIAL TO HAVE A GROWN-UP PRESENT TO MAKE SURE THERE ARE NO ACCIDENTS. Try to follow a few simple rules for best results.

● Read the recipe and make sure you have all the ingredients and equipment needed to make it.

● Tie back long hair, (it's horrid to find a hair in your food). In food shops and restaurant kitchens people wear caps and hats to protect the food.

● Wear a clean apron over your clothes. This is more hygienic and it also protects your clothes from food stains.

● Most important! WASH YOUR HANDS before cooking. Hands are very useful for kneading, mixing, arranging and decorating food, but clean hands are essential each time you handle a different food. This is especially important if handling raw meat, chicken or fish. A different board should be used for raw meat and fish and hands thoroughly washed before preparing salad, sandwiches or other uncooked food.

FOLLOWING A RECIPE
Read the recipe carefully and if you are cooking with a friend, one person can collect the tools and the other can collect the ingredients, otherwise you must do both before you begin. Even the most simple dish can become lumpy or burn if you have to leave it to look for a spoon or fork.
When making cakes, pastry and other baked goods, you must weigh the ingredients accurately. USE EITHER METRIC OR IMPERIAL MEASURES.

SAFETY PRECAUTIONS
1 Do not attempt to lift hot baking sheets or boiling saucepans of pasta or vegetables – ASK FOR HELP. Most accidents happen in the home!

2 Always use proper OVEN GLOVES to touch hot things, even in the microwave oven. Damp tea towels can allow the heat straight through and you can burn fingers or drop the hot dish. If you do have a burn, put under cold running water for as long as it takes someone to prepare a bowl of iced water. Immerse the burned area in the iced water for at least 10 minutes.

3 If you are too small to reach the work surface, make sure you are kneeling on a firm chair. Wobbly stools are dangerous.

4 Do not run in the kitchen in case you slip. Wipe up all spills immediately with a floor cloth or mop.

5 Knives, skewers and blades from food processors are sharp and should never be thrown into the washing up bowl as you or someone else may end up with a cut hand.

6 Do not walk around waving a knife in case you bump into someone. Always use the sharp blade pointing down on a chopping board.

7 Make sure saucepan handles are not sticking out over the cooker as this can be dangerous.

8 Before switching on electric appliances make sure the switch is at OFF. Put in the plug and then switch to ON.

9 Do not plug in or switch on electrical appliances with wet hands.

10 Always check that the lid is securely on blenders or food processors before switching on.

IN THE KITCHEN

When you go to school you need pencils, pens, rubbers and rulers. For cooking, you also need some simple basic equipment and it is helpful to know where the tools you need for each dish are kept in the kitchen.

Before starting to cook, collect the utensils you will need for each dish.

Here is a selection of equipment which will help you prepare the food.

SPOONS

A teaspoon and tablespoon are used a great deal and it is a good idea to keep some specially for cooking. You will find that a set of plastic measuring spoons are quite cheap and are a handy addition to any kitchen as well as being more accurate than ordinary spoons.

A wooden spoon is used to stir hot liquids because metal spoons become hot as heat travels up the handle.

A draining spoon or slotted spoon is a metal spoon with holes. It usually has a long handle and is useful for removing eggs and vegetables from fat or water.

MEASURING JUG

This jug is very useful as it marks out the measures for dry ingredients like sugar and flour on one side; the other side is marked for liquids like water, milk and stock.

SCALES

When you are baking or sweet making it is important to weigh ingredients accurately for a perfect result. Use the handy measures on page 3 if no scales are available or use the measuring jug.

MIXING BOWL

This is a wide deep bowl for mixing which makes sure your food does not spill out. Pyrex-type glass bowls are useful as you can see the mixture and they can also be used in microwave ovens.

CHOPPING BOARDS

These can be made of wood or a white plastic material. It is always better to have two chopping boards. You can use one for meat, fish and vegetables which have to be cooked and the other one for salads, sandwiches and food that will be eaten without further cooking. In this way the ready-to-eat food will not pick up germs from the uncooked food.

KNIVES

Always use knives with great care and ask for help if you have difficulties. Sharp knives are much easier for cutting food; blunt knives make the cutting more difficult and tend to slip.

PALETTE KNIFE

This is a long blade with a round end which is used to pick up flat pieces of food from the frying pan or chopping board. It is also used for icing cakes.

GRATER

Many of these are usefully equipped with several blades for slicing, fine grating and coarse grating.

SQUEEZER

Squeezes all the juice from halved lemons and oranges.

SIEVE

Used for sifting flour, icing sugar and any foodstuff such as sugar which has become lumpy. Also used to strain liquids such as soups and sauces.

COLANDER

Drains water from vegetables and can be used to steam rice and vegetables.

KITCHEN PAPER

Excellent for draining off fat and for covering baked potatoes and bread in the microwave. Also mops up spills.

GREASEPROOF PAPER

Used for lining cake tins.

CLINGFILM & FOIL

Both are useful for wrapping food to store in the fridge or for packed meals. Clingfilm can be used in the microwave but not in the oven and foil can be used in the oven but not in the microwave.

Simply Super Sandwiches

Learn to make a good hearty sandwich before starting on more difficult dishes.

EGG AND HAM SANDWICH

WHAT YOU NEED

Utensils

Bread board
Bowl
Fork
Tablespoon
Wooden spoon
Bread knife
Table knife

Ingredients

4 medium slices bread or rolls
25g/1oz soft margarine or butter
1 egg, hard-boiled
2 tablespoons salad cream
Salt and pepper
Choice of extra fillings
2 slices ham OR 2 slices cooked chicken, chopped OR 1 small can tuna fish, drained OR slices of tomato and cucumber OR 50g/2oz paté OR 4 slices salami or liver sausage OR smoked cheese OR sliced oranges OR apples

What to do

1 Lay the fresh bread slices on the board.

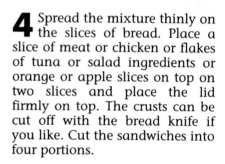

2 Place the butter or margarine in a bowl, add the hard-boiled egg and mash the two ingredients together with a fork. Add the salad cream and mix well with a sprinkling of salt and pepper.

3 Use this as a spread to keep your sandwiches moist and tasty. It also makes a delicious egg sandwich without any other filling.

4 Spread the mixture thinly on the slices of bread. Place a slice of meat or chicken or flakes of tuna or salad ingredients or orange or apple slices on top on two slices and place the lid firmly on top. The crusts can be cut off with the bread knife if you like. Cut the sandwiches into four portions.

5 Serve while fresh or wrap in foil or clingfilm for eating as a packed lunch.

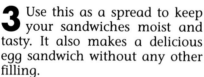

BACON AND EGG PITTA

WHAT YOU NEED

Utensils

Saucepan
Sharp knife
Colander
Tablespoon
Kitchen paper
Bowl
Fish slice

Ingredients

4 wholemeal pitta breads
4 rashers bacon
4 tablespoons mayonnaise
1/2 lettuce
1 bunch mustard and cress
1/4 cucumber
4 hard-boiled eggs
Serves 4

What to do

1 Heat the grill. Cut the rind from the bacon and grill the bacon under a high heat for 2½ minutes each side until it is crisp. Chop neatly. Boil the eggs (page 19).

2 Meanwhile wash the lettuce and cress, draining in a colander. Dice the cucumber.

3 Put the lettuce, mustard and cress and diced cucumber in a bowl with the chopped cooked bacon. Remove the shells from the eggs and cut into quarters. Mix all the ingredients in the bowl with 1 tablespoon mayonnaise and seasoning.

4 Heat the pitta breads under the grill for about 1 minute each side, remove with a fish slice on to four plates. Split the pitta pouches and spread each one with the remaining mayonnaise. Fill with the salad mixture and serve immediately.

Party Sandwiches

Pin wheels
Spread slices of fresh bread without crusts with egg or cream cheese filling. Place a cooked sausage or two gherkins at one end. Roll the bread round the sausage and press to seal the edge. Cut the roll into slices.

Submarine Sandwich
Cut a small French stick into 3 pieces lengthwise and spread each with butter. Fill the bottom with filling, replace the middle slice, fill the top of the middle slice and press firmly. For a party sandwich decorate with flags and a halved tomato as a conning-tower. Cut into slices to serve.

Doorstep sandwiches
Use 2 slices of brown bread with 1 white slice for the centre to give a striped effect. Spread one side of brown with egg mixture and both sides of the middle slice with butter. Put sliced meat, poultry, spicy sausage or cheese in the second layer and top with salad or egg mixture. Top, and cut into triangles.

Cook's Tips

Sandwich Fillings
Use salad vegetables such as lettuce, tomato and cucumber in sandwiches only if they are to be eaten within 1 hour. Watery vegetables soak through the bread making a soggy sandwich.

Carrying sandwiches
Wrap in foil or clingfilm to keep the bread fresh and carry in a box or plastic bag. Do not leave sandwiches on radiators or on window ledges when the sun is shining into a room as even wrapped sandwiches will wilt and become unappetising.

Hot and Tasty
Sandwiches

Hot snacks are always more appealing in cold weather as they make you feel warm from inside!

CROQUE-MONSIEUR

This is a traditional French ham and cheese sandwich that is both delicious and nutritious.

What to do

1 Spread the slices of bread with butter. Place the ham on two of the slices.

2 Grate the cheese into a bowl and sprinkle with pepper and a pinch of paprika, mix the seasoning with the cheese.

3 Divide the cheese equally on top of the ham slices and press the other slices of bread firmly down on top of the cheese.

4 Heat the remaining butter in a frying pan until it sizzles and fry each sandwich for about 2 minutes on each side until the cheese melts. Serve.

Low fat variation

Spread the bread with low fat spread and use half fat cheese for the sandwich. Prepare as directions. Scrape a small amount of low fat spread on the outside of each sandwich. Preheat the grill to hot, turn down to medium and grill the sandwiches for about 2 minutes each side.

WHAT YOU NEED

Utensils

Chopping board
Sharp knife
Grater
Bowl
Plate

Ingredients

4 slices wholemeal bread
50g/2oz cheese
50g/2oz butter
2 slices ham
Pinch of pepper and paprika
Serves 2

BANANA CROISSANTS

This hot snack is fun to make and delicious to eat.

WHAT YOU NEED

Utensils

2 bowls
Fork
Grater
Pastry board or clean work surface
1 baking sheet
1 plastic bag
Rolling pin
Pastry brush

Ingredients

2 bananas
1 lemon
50g/2oz slivered almonds (optional)
50g/2oz amaretti biscuits
308g/11¹/₂oz ready-to-bake croissant dough
Serves 6

What to do

1 Peel the bananas, cut into chunks and mash with a fork in the bowl.

2 Wash and dry the lemon and grate the lemon rind into the banana. Squeeze some juice over the banana to prevent it turning brown.

3 Toast the almonds under the grill until golden. Put the amaretti biscuits into a plastic bag and crush with a rolling pin.

4 Add the almonds and biscuits to the mashed banana and mix well.

5 Heat the oven to 190°C/ 375°F/Gas Mark 5.

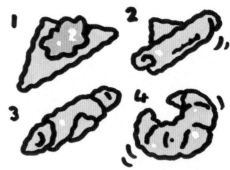

6 Carefully open out the 6 triangles of dough from the can.

7 Spread the banana mixture over the triangles and roll up to form a crescent shape. Place on a greased baking sheet and cook in a hot oven as directed on the wrapper. Serve at once or while still warm.

Cook's Tip
Ready-bake croissants are widely available in many supermarkets.
Savoury Croissants
Grill 6 rashers of bacon until crisp on both sides, crumble and mix with 6 tablespoons grated cheese. Then as 7.

9

pizza

The well loved savoury bread with loads of different toppings to suit everyone.

WHAT YOU NEED

Utensils

Mixing bowl
Plastic bag
Pastry board
Rolling pin
Measuring jug
Teaspoon
Sieve
Flour dredger
Saucer
2 baking sheets
25cm/10 inch
Swiss roll tin

Ingredients

700g/1¹/₂lb strong plain
flour
2 teaspoons salt
2 tablespoons vegetable oil
1 packet ready-mix yeast
450ml/³/₄ pint slightly
warmed water

Makes 3x20cm/8inch
pizzas OR 1x25cm/10inch
oblong pizzas or 4-6
individual rounds

PIZZA DOUGH

What to do

1 Sift the plain flour into the mixing bowl. Add the packet of yeast as directed. Mix well.

2 Add the slightly warmed water and mix well. Knead the mixture on a floured board using the heel of the hand until it is smooth.

3 Place some of the oil in a plastic bag and put the dough in the bag. Leave in a warm atmosphere for at least 1 hour until it is double in size.

4 Turn out the dough on to a floured surface and 'knock back' until smooth again. Divide into two pieces.

5 Roll one half of the dough out until it fits into a 25cm/ 10 inch Swiss roll or oblong tin. Place in the oiled tin and paint the surface with oil. Top with your favourite toppings (see box).

6 Pre-heat the oven 220°C/ 425°F/Gas Mark 7. Brush the top with olive oil and cook for 20 minutes.

7 Roll the remaining half of the dough out thinly and cut into rounds for individual pizzas. Cut around a saucer to shape pizzas.

8 Place on greased baking sheets, brush over with oil and add fillings.

10

Knocking Back Dough

When the yeast dough rises, pockets of gas are formed unevenly throughout and must be "knocked out". Turn the dough on to the floured board and knead with the heel of the hand to make a smooth, elastic dough.

Favourite Toppings

The original pizza was invented for hungry people by the bakers in the back streets of Naples. It was like a hot cheese and tomato open sandwich – a simple piece of dough spread with a tomato base sprinkled with cheese to fill up hungry tummies. Spread the dough with tomato mixture and to top the 20cm/8inch pizza use: 2 finely chopped spring onions, 2 teaspoons chopped basil, 75g/3oz de-rinded streaky bacon, finely chopped and fried with 1 finely sliced onion cooked for 3-4 minutes in a frying pan, 4 chipolata sausages, twisted into 8 halves to top the pizza. Finish pizza with tomato, 8 black olives, stoned and halved. Other toppings you can use: 1x220g/7oz can tomatoes, drained and sliced, 2 slices cooked ham, cut into strips, 50g/2oz thinly sliced mushrooms, 1 small can pineapple slices, 8 green stuffed olives, halved, 1/2 can anchovies, drained and cut in half.
Use double this filling for a large oblong pizza.
Top fillings with 50g/2oz-100g/4oz grated cheese depending on size. Use grated Parmesan, Gruyère, Cheddar or Gloucester.

9 Bake in a pre-heated oven 220°C/425°F Gas Mark 7 until crisp and golden. Check the under-side of large pizzas to make sure they are crisp.

10 Remove from the oven and allow to cool for 3-5 minutes as the fillings retain heat and can burn the mouth. Cut into suitable portions if necessary. Serve with lots of paper napkins or kitchen paper as tomato toppings can be messy.

Pizza Tomato Sauce

To make tomato sauce, place 2-3 tablespoons vegetable oil in a frying pan over a medium heat, add 2 finely chopped onions and 1 grated carrot with 1 crushed clove of garlic. Add 1x400g/14oz can tomatoes and stir until the tomatoes are broken down. Add 2 tablespoons tomato purée, salt, pepper and 1/2 teaspoon of dried basil. Simmer for 25 minutes. You will need about 4 tablespoons of tomato mixture for a 20cm/8inch pizza and 6-7 tablespoons for a 25cm/10inch pizza.
Brush over the pizza base with olive oil and spread on the seasoned tomato mixture. Season with salt, pepper, crushed garlic and chopped fresh oregano, basil or marjoram.

To Bake Pizzas

Heat the oven to 220°C/425°F/Gas Mark 7. New gas ovens do not require a long pre-heat. Place the baking sheets or tin in the oven and bake a large thin pizza for 25-30 minutes. A small individual pizza will cook in about 12 minutes. A deep-dish 20cm/8inch round pizza will bake in about 20 minutes.

Easy Peasy Pizzas

Use French sticks and scone bases to make quick and simple pizzas for snacks and suppers.

QUICK CRUSTY PIZZA

WHAT YOU NEED

Utensils

Bread board
Bread knife
Garlic crusher
Palette knife
Pastry brush
Sharp knife

Ingredients

Long French-style stick
2 tablespoons olive oil
1 clove garlic
4 tomatoes
12 button mushrooms
100g/4oz cheese
100g 4oz lean bacon

Makes 6 snack pizzas

What to do

1 Place the French stick on the board and cut into 3 equal pieces with the bread knife. Cut the pieces of French stick in half.

2 Brush the olive oil on the cut pieces of bread. Crush the garlic and spread along each piece with a palette knife to flavour.

3 Cut the tomatoes and mushrooms into even sliced pieces and cut the cheese into 6-12 slices. Arrange the tomatoes on the bread with the mushrooms on top.

EASY-MIX SCONE PIZZA

WHAT YOU NEED

Utensils

Chopping board
Sharp knife
Saucepan
Wooden spoon
Bowl
Table knife
Tablespoon
Teaspoon
Grater
Can-opener
Rolling pin
Kitchen paper
Greased baking tray

Ingredients

75g/3oz streaky bacon
1 small onion
1 teaspoon vegetable oil
220g/7oz can tomatoes
$1/2$ teaspoon mixed dried herbs
4 pork chipolata sausages
1 tablespoon grated cheese, optional
4 black olives, optional
Scone Pizza Base
225g/8oz self-raising flour
75g/3oz margarine
pinch of salt
1 teaspoon dried mixed herbs
5-6 tablespoons milk
Serves 4

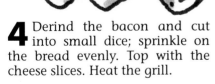

4 Derind the bacon and cut into small dice; sprinkle on the bread evenly. Top with the cheese slices. Heat the grill.

5 Place the bread on the grill pan and cook under a medium heat until golden and bubbly. The cheese will melt and the bacon will be crispy.

What to do

1 Remove any rind from the streaky bacon and cut into small pieces. Chop or grate the onion. Put the oil into a saucepan with the bacon and allow to cook over a medium heat for about 2 minutes.

2 Add the onion and continue cooking over a low heat for about 4 minutes or until the onion is soft but not brown.

3 Drain the tomatoes and stir in with the herbs and a little salt and pepper. Break the tomatoes down with the wooden spoon. Allow the mixture to simmer for 5 minutes, then allow to cool.

4 Twist each sausage into two small sausages by squeezing and twisting in the middle. Grill under a moderate heat until golden, drain on to kitchen paper.

5 Sift the flour into a bowl and rub in the margarine with your fingertips until the mixture looks like breadcrumbs.

6 Stir the herbs into the mixture, add salt and enough milk to make a soft dough. Add the milk gradually as you do not want a sticky dough.

7 Turn the dough onto a floured surface and knead into a smooth round. Roll out into a 20cm/8inch round and place on a greased baking sheet.

8 Heat the oven to 200°C/400°F/Gas Mark 6. Spread the dough with the tomato and bacon mixture. Sprinkle with cheese if using and arrange the sausages on top.

9 Chop or cut the olives in half and arrange on top if using. Cook in a moderately hot oven for 25-30 minutes.

Fresh Or Dried Herbs

For pizzas, pasta sauces and other dishes it is always better to use fresh herbs if you have them in the garden. Now you can also buy them easily in large supermarkets or delicatessens. Chopped basil and oregano with a little parsley give a really good traditional flavour to dishes using lots of tomatoes.

D.I.Y. Burgers

The ever popular burger is at its best when home-made with fresh ingredients such as lean beef, pork or lamb and herbs. Grill, fry or cook on the barbecue when the weather is fine.

BEEFY BURGERS

WHAT YOU NEED

Utensils

Bowl
Grater
Food processor
Chopping board
Knife
Fish slice
Grill pan or frying pan
Pastry brush
Serving plate

Ingredients

225g/8oz lean minced beef
1 small onion
salt and pepper
1 tablespoon fresh breadcrumbs (optional)
2 teaspoons tomato ketchup
1 teaspoon Worcester sauce
2 bap buns, brown or white
Makes 2 quarter pounders

BEEFY BURGERS

What to do

1 Put the lean beef into a bowl with the grated onion on top. Add salt, pepper, breadcrumbs, tomato ketchup and Worcester sauce. If possible, make the breadcrumbs in a food processor, otherwise rub through a sieve. Add all other ingredients and mix for a few seconds to a smoother texture in the food processor or mix the ingredients well in a mixing bowl.

2 Heat the grill until hot, grill the beef burgers for 3 minutes each side on high, then turn the grill down to moderate and grill for 3 minutes each side.

3 Heat the rolls near the grill for 1 minute on each side. Cut in half and put on a plate.

4 Fill the burger bun with any of these – lettuce, tomato, sliced cheese, pickled gherkin, tomato ketchup. Cover with the top of the bun and serve hot.

MONSTER BURGERS

WHAT YOU NEED

Utensils

As for Beefy Burgers

Ingredients

450g/1lb lean minced beef
1 medium onion, grated
25g/1oz fresh breadcrumbs
1 small egg
1 teaspoon tomato ketchup
1 teaspoon Worcester sauce
Salt and pepper
1 level tablespoon flour
4 burger buns
1 tablespoon mild mustard relish
25g/1oz butter
8 small button mushrooms
8 petit pois for eyes
2 processed cheese slices for mouths
Strips of tomatoes for eyebrows
Makes 4 quarter pounders

What to do

1 Mix the beef, onion, breadcrumbs, tomato ketchup and Worcester sauce thoroughly in a bowl with the beaten egg. Season.

2 Roll the mixture into a ball with lightly floured hands. Cut into four even-sized pieces and form into burger shapes.

3 Place under a hot grill for 3 minutes each side, then cook for a further 3 minutes each side under a moderate heat.

4 Divide the butter on the button mushrooms and cook under the grill with the burgers for the last 6 minutes.

5 Spread the buns thinly with relish, place the cooked burger on top and cover with the lids of the roll.

6 Place the mushrooms as two eyes with tomato eyebrows and the cooked peas in the centre of the eyes. Arrange the cheese slices as the monster mouth.

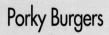

Porky Burgers

Use 450g/1lb lean minced pork in place of the beef. 1 teaspoon mixed herbs can be added to the beef recipe for extra flavour.

Lamburgers

Use 450g/1lb lean minced lamb with 1 tablespoon chopped parsley and 1 teaspoon dried oregano.

Yankee Barbecue
Beans

Favourite foods for parties, campfires and barbecues. A plate, spoon, fork and napkin are all you need to have a bean feast!

BEANS AND BANGERS

What to do

1 Separate the sausages if necessary. Twist each sausage into two and arrange on a grill pan. Prick with a fork.

2 Pre-heat the grill to high for a few minutes.

3 Cut the rind from the bacon and cut the rashers into small squares. Place the rind and the bacon in the casserole and allow to brown over a medium heat.

4 Place the sausages under the grill, making sure that you use oven gloves. Remove the grill pan and place on a steady surface, turn the sausages until they are golden brown on all sides, but not black. Drain on to kitchen paper to remove all of the excess fat.

5 Wash and cut the spring onions into slices and add to the bacon. Allow to cook for about 2 minutes. Remove the bacon rinds and discard.

Creating a casserole

Eating a healthy meal of vegetables and fibre makes good nutritional sense.
Beans and fresh vegetables are excellent for vegetarians – add meat balls (page 22) or sausages to casseroles for those who like meaty dishes.

VEGETABLE CASSEROLE

WHAT YOU NEED

Utensils

As page 16
Colander

Ingredients

8 small carrots, peeled
8 small potatoes, peeled

2 tablespoons oil
4 rashers bacon (optional)
4 sticks celery, sliced
1x200g/7oz can broad beans
1x432g/15oz can red kidney beans
50g/2oz frozen peas (optional) or green beans, mange-tout as liked
2x420g/14oz can baked beans
100g/4oz mushrooms, sliced
Serves 8

What to do

1 Cut the carrots and potatoes in halves. Place in boiling, lightly salted water and cook for 15 minutes, drain through a colander.

2 Heat oil in frying pan and add diced bacon, (optional). Slice the washed celery into thin slices and add to the bacon. Add spring onions, tomatoes, Worcester sauce, tomato ketchup, brown sugar and seasoning as in Yankee Barbecue Beans. Simmer for 15 minutes.

3 Add all the drained vegetables and mushrooms to the casserole. Taste for seasoning.

4 If cooking for vegetarians divide the mixture, retaining more than half in a separate pot. Add 450g/1lb sliced frankfurter sausages or meatballs to the remaining casserole for the non-vegetarians and reheat thoroughly without burning.

6 Add the tomatoes to the casserole with the bacon. Break the tomatoes down with a wooden spoon.

7 Add the sauces, sugar and seasonings. Stir well and add the baked beans and sausages and grated cheese.

8 Reheat in the oven at 180°C/350°F/Gas Mark 4 for 30 minutes or on top of the cooker for at least 10 minutes stirring over a medium heat.

9 Serve with warm wedges of French or wholemeal bread or crispy baked potatoes.

Sunny side up

Cooking eggs is easy if you follow a few simple rules. Unfortunately, eggs become hard and tough if overcooked. Practise and you will soon be able to treat the family to a perfect egg.

EGGY BREAD

WHAT YOU NEED

Utensils

Knife
Bread board
Small bowl
Fork
2 plates
Frying pan
Fish slice
Kitchen paper

Ingredients

2 eggs
Salt and pepper
4 slices of bread
50g/2oz butter
1 tablespoon vegetable oil
Makes 4 slices

What to do

1 Remove the crusts from the bread if liked.

2 Break the eggs into a bowl, add salt and pepper and whisk with a fork.

3 Pour half the mixture on to a plate and put 1 slice of bread in the mixture. Turn the slice over and allow the other side to soak in the egg.

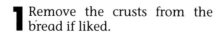

SCRAMBLED EGGS

WHAT YOU NEED

Utensils

Bowl
Saucepan
Fork
Knife
Wooden spoon

Ingredients

25g/1oz butter or low-fat spread
4 eggs
Salt and pepper
2 tablespoons milk
Makes 2 portions

What to do

1 Break the eggs into a bowl add the salt and pepper and whisk with a fork.

2 Melt the fat in the saucepan over a medium heat. Pour in

the beaten eggs and stir with a wooden spoon.

3 When the mixture begins to heat, pour in the measured milk and stir well. Keep stirring the mixture from the bottom of the pan until it sets.

4 Remove from the heat while there is still some liquid left. Stir off the heat and serve hot.

Microwave Scrambled Egg

Use the same ingredients but melt the fat in a bowl for 10 seconds on High. Beat the egg with the milk and seasoning and pour on to the butter. Cook on High for 1 minute, remove from the oven and stir. Return and cook on High for 1 minute. Stir with the wooden spoon and allow to stand covered for 2 minutes.

4 Heat the butter and oil in the frying pan over a medium heat until hot. Place 2 slices of eggy bread in the pan and cook until golden each side, turning once. Drain on kitchen paper.

5 Add the remaining egg to the plate and continue preparing the other two slices. Fry until golden on both sides.

Serve with grilled bacon, grilled tomatoes, fried or grilled mushrooms, sausages or even fried eggs to make the breakfast or supper of your choice.

Hard and Soft Boiled eggs

Don't wait for a surprise when you take the top from your boiled egg. Make sure it is just right by using your watch or a timer.
Have a small saucepan on a medium heat with enough boiling water to cover the egg. Lower the egg into the water slowly, on a spoon, without dropping it, and cook for 4¹/₂ minutes. This will give you a soft-boiled egg to eat with your toast fingers. This method will cook an egg straight out of the fridge and a newly laid egg.
Eggs which have been in a rack in the kitchen or larder will cook in 4 minutes.
To cook hard-boiled eggs simply boil for 8-12 minutes depending on the size. Put cold water into the saucepan over the eggs to prevent them becoming grey around the yolk.

Real Poached Eggs

Fill a frying pan half-full of water. Bring the water to simmering point (not to boiling point or the eggs will toughen). Break the egg into a cup and slide the egg into the pan. Baste the eggs carefully by splashing a spoonful of water over the yolk. Prepare a plate with some crumpled kitchen paper on it. Remove the egg from the pan with a slotted spoon and place on the paper to drain. Remove on to a heated plate and serve with toast.

Fried Eggs

Heat 1 tablespoon oil in a non-stick frying pan over a medium heat. Break the eggs into a cup and slide into the pan, cook for 2-3 minutes until set. Remove with a fish slice and serve on warm plates or use in rolls for a quick breakfast.

Break an Egg

Many easy and filling recipes are made with eggs apart from the usual breakfast or high tea dishes on page 19. Make an omelette, add a variety of fillings for hearty appetites or try Potato and Cheese Pie.

OMELETTE

WHAT YOU NEED

Utensils

20cm/8inch omelette or frying pan
Bowl
Fork
Palette knife

Ingredients

2 eggs
3 teaspoons cold water
Salt and pepper
25g/1oz butter or margarine

Suggested fillings

1 sliced tomato
1 slice chopped ham
25g/1oz grated cheese
2 rashers of bacon, grilled
1 teaspoon mixed herbs
2 tablespoons mixed chopped tomato, parsley, spring onion and pepper
Makes 1 omelette

What to do

1 Break the eggs into a bowl with the salt, pepper and water. Whisk until slightly frothy with a fork.

2 Melt the butter or margarine in an omelette or frying pan. Pour in the eggs when the butter begins to sizzle.

3 Pull the cooked mixture from the sides to the middle of the omelette pan to allow the mixture to run to the outside and set.

4 The omelette is cooked when the bottom is golden brown and the top is like very soft scrambled egg. Add any filling or mixture of fillings at this stage.

5 Flip over half the omelette with the palette knife, and slide on to a heated plate. Serve with salad and oven chips or a chunky piece of bread.

OVEN POTATO AND CHEESE PIE

WHAT YOU NEED

Utensils

20-25cm/8-10inch ovenproof dish
Brush
Large saucepan
Grater
Chopping board
Sharp knife
Fork
Measuring jug
Colander

Ingredients

1.5kg/3¹/₄lbs new potatoes
15g/¹/₂oz butter or margarine
50g/2oz cheese
2 large eggs
450ml/³/₄pint milk
Salt and pepper
1 tablespoon chopped chives or parsley
Serves 4

What to do

1 Wash or scrub the potatoes and put in boiling salted water. Cook for about 15-20 minutes until tender but still firm. Drain in a colander.

2 Preheat the oven to 190°C/375°F/Gas Mark 5. Butter the ovenproof dish all over.

3 Grate the cheese and cut the potatoes when slightly cooled into thin slices. Arrange a layer of potatoes in the dish then sprinkle with a layer of cheese and then arrange another layer of potatoes. Keep 1 tablespoon of cheese for sprinkling on top.

4 Beat the eggs together with salt, pepper and milk. Pour the mixture of eggs and milk over the potatoes. Sprinkle with the remaining cheese and bake for 20-25 minutes until the top is golden brown and the egg mixture has set.

5 Sprinkle with chives or parsley and serve with a crisp salad.

Cook's Tip

If you find you have dropped some shell into the egg then remove it easily by using the half of an eggshell which will attract the small piece of shell rather like a magnet.

Perfect Pasta

WHAT YOU NEED

Utensils

Mixing bowl
Grater
Chopping board
Wooden spoon
Large saucepan
Frying pan
Tablespoon
Teaspoon
Plate
1 sharp knife or a pair of scissors
Can-opener

Ingredients

225g/8oz lean minced beef
1 small onion
1 tablespoon parsley
Salt and pepper
1 tablespoon flour
2 tablespoons oil

Sauce
1 small onion
1 small carrot
400g/14oz can tomatoes
150ml/¼pint water
2 teaspoons cornflour
1 tablespoon tomato purée
½ teaspoon basil

350g/12oz pasta
Salt and pepper
25g/1oz butter
Pinch of nutmeg
Serves 4

Easy to cook, nutritious and healthy to eat. Have it hot with a delicious sauce or cold in a salad.

MEAT BALLS WITH PASTA

What to do

1 Put the meat into a mixing bowl. Grate the onion into the bowl. Chop the parsley with a sharp knife or cut into small pieces with scissors into the bowl.

2 Add some salt and pepper and mix together well. (For a really smooth mixture you can blend in a food processor for 30 seconds).

3 Sprinkle the flour on to the chopping board and dust over the hands.

4 Divide the mixture into 12 pieces and roll into equal-sized balls. Heat the oil in a frying pan on a medium heat and fry the meat balls until golden brown turning frequently. Drain on to a piece of kitchen paper crumpled on a plate.

TOMATO PASTA SALAD

WHAT YOU NEED

Utensils

Large saucepan
Colander
1 sharp knife
1 salad bowl
Clean screw top jar
Tablespoon

Ingredients

250g/8oz pasta shapes
8 cherry tomatoes
2 large tomatoes
1 small courgette
1/2 cucumber
2 spring onions

Dressing
4 tablespoons olive oil
1 tablespoon wine vinegar
1 clove garlic
1 tablespoon basil leaves or parsley
Salt and pepper
Serves 4

What to do

1 Cook the pasta as directed in box below. Small shapes will take about 5 minutes. Drain and rinse in a colander with cold water and then drain well again.

2 Cut the cherry tomatoes in half and put into the large salad bowl. Add the cold pasta.

3 Place the large tomatoes into boiling water on the end of a fork. Remove and the skin will peel off. Cut into halves and then into wedges. Add to the bowl and mix again with the pasta.

4 Wash the cucumber and courgette and dry well with kitchen paper. Cut into thin slices. Add the slices to the bowl.

5 Put the oil and vinegar into a screw top jar. Crush the garlic and add to the jar. Chop the herbs with a knife or with scissors and add to the jar. Screw on the top firmly and shake the jar vigorously until well mixed.

6 Pour on to the salad and allow to stand for at least 15 minutes before serving.

5 To make the sauce, grate the onion and carrot and cook over a low heat in the same pan as used for the meat balls.

6 Add the tomatoes with the juice and half the water to the pan. Break the tomatoes by stirring with a wooden spoon.

7 Mix the cornflour with the remaining water, the tomato purée and basil. Stir this into the sauce until it thickens. For a smoother sauce you can put the mixture through the food processor or blender. Add some salt and pepper, basil and nutmeg, then taste the sauce for flavour.

8 Place the meat balls in the sauce, cover and cook gently on a low heat for 20 minutes.

Cooking Pasta

A large saucepan should be slightly more then half-filled with water. Add 1 teaspoon salt and a few drops of vegetable oil. When the water comes to the boil, feed the pasta in, gradually stirring with a wooden spoon or fork. Allow to cook for the time suggested in the directions given on the packet. Dried spaghetti takes about 12 minutes, thin noodles take less time. Drain the pasta in to a colander when cooked and return to the pan with a knob of butter and a little pepper. Shake gently over a low heat and serve with sauce and meatballs. Grated cheese may be served in a separate dish.

Spicy Dips with

Strips

Scrumptious savoury chicken pieces are quick to prepare and cook. Serve at parties and barbecues.

stalks and then cut into sticks about the same length as match sticks. Cut the cucumber into chunks and the tomatoes into quarters or halves, depending on the size. Arrange all the vegetables on a dish, cover with cling-film until the chicken is cooked.

What to do

1 Place the chicken on a chopping board and carefully slice it into even-sized pieces.

2 Sprinkle the flour on to a plate and dip the chicken strips into the flour. Shake off excess flour and put on a clean plate. Leave in the fridge until you are ready to cook the chicken.

3 Clean the chopping board and clear away the flour. Prepare the vegetables for cutting into sticks.

4 Cut the peeled carrots into slices and then into sticks. Remove strings from the celery

5 To make the peanut dip, mix all the ingredients in a medium-sized mixing bowl. Squeeze the orange and add juice for flavour.

6 In a medium-sized mixing bowl place the fromage frais or yogurt, tomato and other ingredients. Mix well, sprinkle with some of the chopped chives.

7 Place both dips in attractive dishes with the vegetable sticks arranged around them. Store in the fridge.

8 Heat the oil in an non-stick frying pan and fry the chicken strips until golden and cooked through (about 5 minutes). Drain on kitchen paper. Serve on the plate with dips.

Chicken Picnics

Popular chicken pieces are firm favourites for picnics and packed meals.

PEANUT CHICKEN PASTIES

WHAT YOU NEED

Utensils

Bowl
Sieve
Saucepan
Foil
Tablespoon
Whisk
Chopping board
Sharp knife
Can-opener
2 baking sheets
Pastry brush
Pastry board
Fish slice
Rolling pin
Wire rack

Ingredients

225g/8oz flour
75g/3oz hard margarine
4 tablespoons peanut butter

For the Filling
25g/1oz margarine or butter
25g/1oz plain flour
300ml/$^1/_2$ pint milk
Salt and pepper
225g/8oz cooked chicken
100g/4oz canned or frozen sweetcorn
3 spring onions
2 tablespoons milk
Serves 4

What to do

1 Sift the flour into the bowl, rub in the margarine with the fingertips until the mixture is like fine breadcrumbs.

2 Add the peanut butter and mix well adding a few drops of cold water gradually until the mixture makes a fairly soft dough. Wrap in foil and put in fridge for 10 minutes.

3 Put the milk, fat and flour into a saucepan and place over a medium heat, whisk all the time as the mixture heats. The sauce will become smooth and thick. Add salt and pepper.

4 Remove from the heat and allow to cool for about 5 minutes, whisk occasionally.

5 Chop the chicken into dice. Wash and chop the spring onions. Add chicken, sweetcorn, spring onions and salt and pepper to the sauce, mixing well. Allow to cool.

6 When the pastry and filling are prepared heat the oven to 190°C/375°F/Gas Mark 5. Grease 2 baking sheets by rubbing with a butter wrapper or vegetable oil.

CHICKEN NUGGETS WITH ORANGEY PEANUT DIP

WHAT YOU NEED

Utensils

1 baking sheet
Tablespoon
Lemon squeezer
Bowl
Grater
Kitchen paper

Ingredients

450g/1lb
chicken nuggets or bites
Sauce
5 tablespoons smooth peanut
butter
4 tablespoons Greek yogurt
3 tablespoons orange juice
1 tablespoon chopped peanuts
1 teaspoon orange rind
Serves 4

What to do

1 Heat the grill or the oven as directed on the chicken bites and grill or bake as directed.

2 Drain the chicken on a piece of kitchen paper.

3 Mix the peanut butter, yogurt and orange juice in a small bowl until smooth. Sprinkle with chopped peanuts and thin strips of orange rind.

4 Serve the chicken nuggets hot or cold with the sauce and a crisp salad.

Cook's Tip

For packed lunches or picnics, carry pasties in a plastic box otherwise they will squash on the journey. Eat with a juicy tomato or a mixed salad.

7 Divide the pastry in to 4 pieces and roll into smooth balls. Lightly flour a rolling pin and roll out to 13-15cm/5-6 inches in diameter.

8 Place 2-3 tablespoons of filling on one side and brush the edges of the pastry with milk. Press the edges together and place on a greased baking sheet, brush the top with milk.

9 Make the other 3 pastry balls into pasties, arrange on 2 baking sheets, brush with milk and bake for 25 minutes until golden brown.

10 Remove from the trays on to a wire rack to cool. Eat hot or cold.

Barbecued Sweet and Sour Drumsticks

Place a new, large plastic freezer bag in a bowl. Pour in 4 tablespoon red wine vinegar, 2 tablespoons tomato purée, 2 tablespoons soy sauce, 2 tablespoons clear honey, 1 tablespoon Worcester sauce, 2 cloves of garlic, crushed, 1 teaspoon cayenne pepper, salt and pepper. Squeeze the plastic bag to mix the ingredients. Replace in the bowl and add 8 plump chicken drumsticks. Mix well with the marinade and seal in the bag. Place the bag in a bowl in the fridge for several hours or up to 24 hours. Turn the bag from time to time to move the mixture round the chicken. Cook on the barbecue for at least 25 minutes or grill for 8-10 minutes each side. Serve hot or eat cold as a picnic or packed meal.
Serves 8

Jolly Jackets

Baked jacket potatoes are ideal with butter as a vegetable or stuffed for a meal – favourites at bonfire, Hallowe'en and barbecue parties.
Use 1 baking potato per person, unless they are very large, then half a stuffed potato will be enough.

WHAT YOU NEED

Utensils

Fork
Frying pan
Can-opener
Wooden spoon
Potato masher
Knife
Tongs or fish slice
Bowl
Tablespoon
Baking sheet

Ingredients

6 baking potatoes
450g/1lb lean minced pork
227g/8oz can barbecue beans
Salt and pepper
1 tablespoon tomato ketchup
50g/2oz butter or low fat spread
2-4 tablespoons milk
100g/4oz grated cheese
Serves 6

PORKY BAKED POTATOES

What to do

1 Pre-heat the oven to 200°C, 400°F, Gas Mark 6.

2 Take the fork in one hand and hold each potato firmly with the other hand and prick the potatoes all over with the fork. Lift them with tongs or a fish slice and place them on the oven shelf, making sure that your hands are protected.

3 Bake the potatoes for 1 hour depending on size. If they are large they will need longer.

4 Fifteen minutes before the potatoes are cooked, put the frying pan on a medium heat. Add the minced pork and stir carefully until it separates and is golden brown (no fat is needed).

5 Add the beans with some salt, pepper and tomato ketchup and allow to simmer on a very low heat until the potatoes are prepared.

6 Cut the potatoes in half, holding with oven gloves. Scoop the potato middle with a spoon into a bowl and mash together with the butter and milk.

7 Remove the meat from the heat and place the halved potatoes on a baking sheet. Fill the shells with the meat mixture.

8 Divide the mashed potatoes evenly into 12 portions and spoon onto the meat, smooth.

9 Sprinkle with cheese and return to the oven for 20 minutes on the baking sheet.

Quicky Potatoes

If you have a microwave oven this will save fuel.
To cook in the microwave follow these instructions.
Prick potatoes all over.
One potato will cook in 5-6 minutes on High. Two potatoes will cook in 10-12 minutes. Six potatoes will cook in 30 minutes.
For a crispy outside, place in the oven for 10 minutes before removing the inside to fill. Brown in the oven or under a grill after filling. Handle with oven gloves as the potatoes will be very hot when they are removed from the microwave oven.

Favourite Fillings

Tuna and Cheese Potatoes
Bake potatoes as described in Porky Baked Potatoes. Scoop the inside of the potato into the bowl and mash with butter and milk. Add 1 tablespoon chopped parsley and 1 tablespoon chopped chives. Mix well, then add 100g/4oz grated double Gloucester cheese with 1x 200g/7oz can drained tuna fish and 1 tablespoon thawed, cooked or canned sweet corn. Pile the mixture back into the potato skins and sprinkle with more grated cheese. Cook for 20 minutes.

Baked Beans and Bacon
Cook the potatoes as in the recipe. Mash the potatoes with butter, milk and seasoning.
Fill the shells with heated baked beans and top with mashed potatoes. Cook four slices of bacon on a baking tray in the oven when re-heating the potatoes for the last 20 minutes. Serve the bacon on top of the beans.

Crisp Salads

Experiment with different salad ingredients to make quick, easy and healthy meals.

What to do

1 Place the eggs in the a saucepan of cold water and bring to the boil for 10 minutes. Then put under a cold running tap for 30 seconds and leave to cool in the cold water.

2 Turn the grill on to high, cut the rind from the bacon and cook under the grill for two minutes each side. Turn the grill down to medium when the bacon is turned over. Cook until crispy, drain on kitchen paper.

3 Remove the crusts from the bread and cut into 2.3mm/ $1/2$ inch squares. Heat 2 tablespoons oil in the frying pan, crush the garlic and add to the oil. Spread over the pan and add the bread. Fry until golden, turning over after a few seconds. Drain the croûtons on to kitchen paper.

SUNSHINE SALAD

WHAT YOU NEED

Utensils

Colander
Saucepan
Kitchen paper
Chopping board
Frying pan
Sharp knife
Serving dish
Garlic crusher
Screwtop jar
Tablespoon
Teaspoon
Wooden spoon

Ingredients

4 eggs
225g/8oz bacon
6 tablespoons olive oil
2 cloves garlic
2 slices white bread
6 ripe tomatoes
100g/4oz mushrooms
$1/2$ cucumber
175g/6oz spinach leaves
1 small lettuce
2 tablespoons vinegar
$1/2$ teaspoon mustard
2 teaspoons honey
Salt and pepper
Serves 4

4 On a clean chopping board, slice the tomatoes and arrange carefully around the edge of the dish.

5 Wash the mushrooms and cucumber and cut into slices. Wash the spinach and lettuce, drain in the colander.

6 Arrange the mushrooms, lettuce and cucumber and spinach leaves in the centre of the dish.

7 Remove the shells from the eggs and cut in half or wedges, as you like. Arrange in the centre of the dish and sprinkle with the crispy bacon.

8 In the screwtop jar, put 4 tablespoons olive oil, the vinegar, mustard, honey, salt and pepper. Put the top on the jar and shake well, dress the salad just before serving.

9 Sprinkle the crisp croûtons over the salad.

Cook's tip
Do not add dressing, mayonnaise or salad cream to salads which have lettuce, spinach or chicory until you are ready to serve or the leaves will become soggy.
It is often more economical to serve the dressing separately and then left-over salad can be stored in a plastic box in the fridge.

SALAMI AND POTATO SALAD

WHAT YOU NEED

Utensils

Saucepan
Colander
Teaspoon
Tablespoon
Chopping board
Sharp knife
Scissors
Bowl
Serving dish

Ingredients

675g/1¹/₂lbs salad potatoes
7floz/200mls soured cream
6 tablespoons mayonnaise
Salt and pepper
1 teaspoon English mustard
1 bunch of chives
¹/₂ cucumber
1 red pepper or large tomato
1 frisée or other frilly lettuce
225g/8oz Italian salami slices
2 spring onions
Serves 4-6

What to do

1 Wash and boil the potatoes until tender. Drain in the colander and place under a cold running tap to cool.

2 In a bowl, mix the soured cream with the mayonnaise, salt, pepper and mustard. Add potatoes.

3 Wash and cut the chives with a pair of scissors or sharp knife. Add to the potato mixture.

4 Chop the cucumber into dice, add to the bowl; mix.

5 Cut the pepper in half and remove seeds, then cut into thin slices.

6 Wash the lettuce and drain in the colander. Arrange on a large serving dish.

7 Tip the potato mixture carefully into the centre of the dish and arrange salami slices on top.

8 Wash and chop spring onions into small circles and sprinkle on top of the salad.

Shape up a Biscuit

Baking biscuits is lots of fun and a great way to spend a rainy afternoon.

CRUNCHY GINGERBREAD MEN

What to do

1 Sift the flour, bicarbonate of soda and ginger into a bowl.

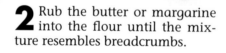

WHAT YOU NEED

Utensils

Scales
Mixing bowl
Sieve
Pastry board
Flour dredger
Wooden spoon
Teaspoon
Tablespoon
Rolling pin
Gingerbread man cutter
2 baking sheets
Piping bag
Wire cooling tray
Writing icing nozzle

Ingredients

350g/12oz plain flour
1 level teaspoon
bicarbonate soda
2 level teaspoons ground
ginger
100g/4 oz hard margarine
or butter
175g/6oz Demerara sugar
4 level tablespoons golden
syrup
1 egg
Serves 6

To decorate
Currants
50g/2oz glacé icing

2 Rub the butter or margarine into the flour until the mixture resembles breadcrumbs.

3 Stir in the sugar and then take a wooden spoon and beat in the syrup and the egg.

4 Sprinkle a little flour on the board, turn the dough out and knead until smooth.

5 Pre-heat the oven to 190°C/375°F/Gas Mark 5. Grease the baking sheets by brushing with a little oil or rubbing over with a buttered paper.

6 Roll out the dough with a lightly floured rolling pin to 5mm/¼inch thickness. Cut the shapes with the cutter and arrange with space between them on the baking trays.

7 Make buttons and eyes by pressing the currants into the mixture and cook in the oven for about 12 minutes.

8 Remove the trays with oven gloves and place the biscuits on wire trays to cool.

9 Make up the glacé icing (see page 35) with a few drops of warm water. Put the icing in the bag and mark the mouth with the pipe with white icing. If you enjoy piping, you can draw hands and feet on to the biscuits as well.

32

FACE BISCUITS

WHAT YOU NEED

Utensils

As for
Gingerbread Men
Tablespoon
Fork
Cup
Sharp knife
Palette knife
15cm/2inch plain cutter
Plastic bag

Ingredients

100g/4oz hard margarine
100g/4oz caster sugar
1 egg
250g/8oz plain flour
To Decorate
250g/8oz icing sugar
1 tablespoon cocoa
Glacé cherries
Currants
Shredded coconut
Yellow food colouring
Flaked almonds
Makes 20 biscuits

What to do

1 Put the margarine and caster sugar into a bowl and cream with a wooden spoon until the mixture is light in colour and slightly fluffy in appearance.

2 Break the egg into a cup and beat it lightly with a fork. Add to the bowl and beat the mixture with 1 tablespoon flour.

3 Sieve the flour into the bowl and mix to a soft dough with clean hands.

4 Dust the board lightly with flour and turn out the dough. Knead lightly and roll out to 5mm/¼ inch thick.

5 Pre-heat the oven to 180°C/ 350°F/Gas Mark 4, Rub over the baking sheets with a little vegetable oil on a piece of kitchen paper.

6 Cut the biscuits into 5cm/2inch rounds, place on

the baking sheet with a little space between each. Bake for 10-12 minutes until pale golden.

7 Allow to cool on the tray for a few minutes and then move the biscuits on to a wire rack with a palette knife to cool and harden.

8 Wash the bowl and put half the icing sugar into one bowl and the remainder into the other bowl with the cocoa. Mix each batch of icing with a little warm water until thick but still falling from the spoon.

9 Cover half the biscuits with white icing and half with chocolate icing. Make the faces on the biscuits by using cherries for the mouths, currants and almonds for the eyes.

10 To make the hair put half the coconut in a plastic bag with a few drops of yellow colouring. Rub the bag between the hands to mix the colour into the coconut.

11 Use the yellow hair for the white biscuits and the remaining white coconut for the chocolate iced biscuits. Allow to dry for 30 minutes before eating.

Quick and Easy Flapjacks

Grease a 28cm/11inch-18cm/ 7inch tin and heat the oven to 190°C/375°F/ Gas Mark 5. In a saucepan melt 100g/4oz hard margarine, 4 level tablespoons golden syrup and 50g/2oz soft brown sugar over a low heat. When well mixed and the sugar has dissolved add 175g/6oz rolled oats, ½ teaspoon mixed spice and the finely grated rind of one orange mixing well. Bake in the oven for 25-30 minutes. Cut into fingers while still warm. Drizzle melted chocolate on top.

Yummy Cakes

ALL-IN-ONE SPONGE CAKE

WHAT YOU NEED

Utensils

Scales
Bowl
Wooden spoon
Teaspoon
Tablespoon
20cm/8inch non-stick sandwich cake tin
Sieve
Plastic spatula
Cup
Wire cooling rack
Pastry brush

Ingredients

125g/4oz soft margarine
125g/4oz caster sugar
125g/4oz self-raising flour
1 teaspoon baking powder
2 eggs
1 teaspoon oil
Serves 8

Cakes are fun, if messy to make, but well worth the effort! Practise icing on bought sponge cakes.

What to do

1 Pre-heat the oven to 180°C/350°F/Gas Mark 4.

2 Measure the margarine and sugar into the bowl. Sift the flour and baking powder.

3 Break the eggs into a cup, drop into the bowl. Add one tablespoon warm water.

4 With the wooden spoon, mix all the ingredients together and beat for one minute.

5 Grease the sandwich tin by brushing with oil or using buttered paper.

6 Scrape the sponge mixture into the tin with the spatula.

7 Bake in the oven for 25-30 minutes or until pale golden.

8 Allow to cool for 5 minutes in the tin. Carefully, with oven gloves, turn out on to the wire rack and allow to cool.

Variation

To make a marble ring. Prepare the cake as left with 175g/6oz flour, sugar, margarine and 3 eggs. Grease a ring mould tin and heat the oven, as before. Divide the cake mixture in two, on each side of the bowl. Blob half the mixture in different places in the tin, leaving spaces between each spoonful. Mix one tablespoon of cocoa powder with two tablespoons warm water in a cup and add to the remaining cake mixture, mixing well. Spoon the chocolate cake mixture between the plain mixture already in the tin. Bang the cake tin on the table to even the mixture. Cook until the top of the sponge springs back when touched, approximately 25 minutes. Allow to cool for 5 minutes and then turn out on to a wire rack. When cool, drizzle glacé icing over the top.

DOUGAL CAKE

WHAT YOU NEED

Utensils

Bowl
Wooden spoon
Tablespoon
Teaspoon
Sieve
Piping bag
Piping nozzle
Oblong plate
Palette knife
Cup

Ingredients

1 ready-made Swiss roll
75g/3oz butter or margarine
250g/8oz icing sugar
2 tablespoons cocoa
2 tablespoons milk
Few drops vanilla essence
Glacé icing
50g/2oz icing sugar
Smarties and chocolate drops
Serves 6

What to do

1 Put the Swiss roll on an oblong plate.

2 Soften the butter or margarine with the wooden spoon, sift in icing sugar, mixing gradually.

3 Put the cocoa in a cup and mix well with the milk and vanilla essence.

4 Add to the icing sugar and mix well until you have a soft, creamy icing.

5 Spoon the icing into a bag with a rose nozzle. Pipe half loops from the middle of the Swiss roll to the plate to make Dougal's coat.

6 Make the glacé icing by adding a few drops of warm water to the 50g/2oz icing sugar and mixing well.

7 Cover each end of the Dougal cake with glacé icing with the palette knife, and arrange the Smarties and chocolate drops to make his face, add more to the body if liked.

Cook's Tip
If you do not have a pipe and piping bag, spread the icing over the Swiss roll with a palette knife and make the coat pattern by marking with a fork from the middle to the plate.

Easy Finishes
Split the sandwich cake, spread the centre with jam and put the two halves together. Sprinkle with the sieved icing sugar. For a fancy design place a paper doiley over the cake and sprinkle the icing sugar. Carefully remove the paper and you will find the icing sugar has formed patterns. Alternatively, sandwich together with butter icing and spread some on top. Smooth with a palette knife then make a pattern using a fork. Cakes can also be filled with fresh fruit and whipped cream.

Caterpillar

Meringues

The ideal celebration cake for special occasions. No messy cutting up, one or two segments of caterpillar serves one. Cook the meringue shells in the microwave to save time. Makes 20 individual shells.

MICROWAVE MERINGUES

WHAT YOU NEED

Utensils

Pencil
1 piece greaseproof or non-stick paper
Measuring jug
Metal spoon
Medium-sized bowl
Microwave oven
Scissors

Ingredients

200g/7oz Microwave Meringue Mix
20ml/4 teaspoons cold water
Few drops green and red food colouring

What to do

1 Place the microwave turntable on the greaseproof paper and draw a circle around it. Cut out the circle.

2 Measure half the water into the bowl and sprinkle half the meringue mix over the top. Stir with a metal spoon until the mixture binds together.

3 Wash and dry your hands well and bring the mixture together with your finger-tips. Knead the dough until it is smooth and glossy.

4 Divide the dough into 10 pieces and roll into balls with the palm of your hand.

TRADITIONAL MERINGUES

WHAT YOU NEED

Utensils

Large mixing bowl
Whisk or electric whisk
Spatula
Scales
Tablespoon
2 baking sheets
2 sheets non-stick paper
Wire rack
2 dessertspoons or
piping bag and tube

Ingredients

4 egg whites (medium)
1/2 teaspoon cream of tartar
or salt
225g/8oz caster sugar
4 drops vanilla essence
Makes 16 shells

What to do

1 Place the egg whites in a bowl with the cream of tartar or salt. Whisk until just stiff and can stand in peaks.

2 Sprinkle in 4 tablespoons caster sugar, one spoon at a time while whisking the mixture and until it becomes shiny and glossy. This will take about 30 seconds and the meringue will form shallow peaks.

3 Using the spatula, gently fold in the remaining sugar, adding a few tablespoons at a time with the vanilla essence. Fold in until the meringue forms peaks. (It is important not to whisk at this stage.).

4 Heat the oven to a very low temperature 120°C/250°F/Gas Mark 1/2. Place the paper on the baking sheets.

5 Make the shell-shapes on the non-stick paper by placing the mixture with two dessert spoons or through a large piping bag and tube, allowing enough space to spread.

6 Bake for 1-1 1/2 hours until crisp. The meringue should stay white or only turn the palest beige. If the meringue is browning, turn the oven down and leave the door slightly ajar.

7 Cool on a wire tray and sandwich together with whipped cream or butter cream.

Creating the Caterpillar

Utensils

Bowl
Wooden spoon
Sieve
Grater

Fillings
5floz/1/4 pint whipping cream or butter cream

Butter Cream

Ingredients

175g/6oz butter or margarine, softened
175/6oz icing sugar
Grated rind of 1 lemon
1 teaspoon lemon juice
Sweets for decoration

What to do

1 Either sandwich the meringues together with whipped cream or make butter cream. Cream together the butter, icing sugar, lemon rind and juice.

2 Sandwich together alternate coloured meringues.

3 Use a dab of butter cream to sandwich caterpillar together. Arrange on a board and decorate with sweets.

5 Arrange the 10 balls 5cm/ 2 inches apart in a circle on the paper circle placed on the microwave turntable.

6 Microwave on High for 1 minute 30 seconds (in a 650 Watt oven). Allow to stand for 3 minutes. Transfer on to a wire rack to cool.

7 When making the coloured meringues, first mix 1 tea-spoon of water with a few drops of red food colouring in a bowl. Add 50g/2oz meringue mix and prepare as in step 4, making five balls of pink meringue.

8 Place on the microwave turntable, cook as in step 6.

9 Meanwhile mix 1 teaspoon water with a few drops of green colouring in the bowl. Add 50g/2oz of the meringue mix, knead and make into 5 green balls, and cook as in step 6.

An apple a day

Enjoy apples, fresh and crisp, after lunch or supper and remember to take one with your packed lunch. Make this special treat for Bonfire night.

Toffee Apples

WHAT YOU NEED

Utensils

**10 lolly sticks or
10x13cm/5 inch wooden
skewers
Scales
Kitchen paper
Thick-bottomed saucepan
Washing-up bowl
Wooden spoon
Sugar thermometer
(optional)
Tablespoon
Knife
Measuring jug
Baking tray
Non-stick paper**

Ingredients

**8 medium crisp dessert
apples
450g/1lb Demerara sugar
50g/2oz butter
1 teaspoon vinegar
1¹/₂tbsp golden syrup
150 ml/¹/₄ pint water
Makes 8**

What to do

1 Wash the apples and wipe dry with kitchen paper. Allow to stand after wiping before dipping in the toffee or it will not stick. Gently push the sticks into the apples. Place on a tray.

2 Tip the sugar, butter, vinegar, golden syrup and water into a heavy saucepan. Place over a very gentle heat until the sugar has dissolved completely.

3 When all the sugar has dissolved, increase the heat and boil the sugar mixture in the saucepan rapidly for about 5-8 minutes. This is about 143°C/290°F if using a sugar thermometer or until it is at soft crack stage.

4 Very carefully place the saucepan into the bowl or a basin which has hot water in it. Take care the water does not splash into the toffee. This will keep the toffee soft until all the apples are dipped.

5 Using the stick as a handle dip the apples in the toffee, turning until the excess toffee drips off.

6 Place each apple on a buttered tray or line the tray with non-stick paper first.

7 Allow to cool and set hard before eating.

This recipe should only be made with the help of a grown-up.

Cook's Tips

- Always use oven gloves for hot saucepans. Make sure a grown-up is with you when you make sweets as boiling sugar is dangerous if spilled.
- For sweet-making all the ingredients should be weighed out accurately.
- The sugar must be dissolved completely before boiling.
- Remember to wash or wipe the apples at least half an hour before dipping in toffee.
- Use firm crisp apples as the temperature of the toffee is high. A soft apple will become mushy if used.
- Do not stir the boiling toffee or it will crystallise.

Testing Boiled Sugar Mixtures

It can be quite difficult to judge when boiled sugar mixtures are at the correct temperature. The easiest way to do this if you intend to make lots of sweets for bazaars, fund-raising or presents is to buy a sugar thermometer. This will make it easier to ensure that the temperature of the mixture is right. However with care this simple test can be done.
Prepare a bowl of iced water and drop a small spoonful of mixture into the water. If it forms a firm ball it will caramelise in the remaining heat. Remove from the heat at this stage or the mixture will turn into caramel and will be difficult to use.

Sweets

Super fudge for all occasions. Make sure you have a grown-up with you when making sweets.

EASY FUDGE

WHAT YOU NEED

Utensils

Scales
Tablespoon
Can-opener
Teaspoon
Large saucepan
Sugar thermometer
(optional)
Wooden spoon
Electric hand-mixer
(optional)
Sharp knife
18cm/7in square tin
Air-tight plastic box or tin

Ingredients

450/1lb granulated sugar
50g/2oz butter or
margarine
2 tablespoon golden syrup
4 tablespoons water
8 tablespoons condensed
milk
1/2 teaspoon vanilla
flavouring
Makes 49 pieces

What to do

1 Put the sugar, butter or margarine, golden syrup, water and condensed milk into a thick-bottomed saucepan. Place on a low heat, stirring from time to time until the sugar dissolves.

2 When all the sugar has dissolved bring the mixture to the boil. Do not stir at this stage. Continue boiling until the soft ball stage is reached. If using a sugar thermometer, remove from heat when the temperature reaches 116°C/240°F. Otherwise test a spoonful of mixture in iced water until a soft ball forms.

3 Put the saucepan on a firm surface and beat the fudge with a wooden spoon or an electric hand-mixer. As the mixture is beaten it will become thick and grainy. Add the vanilla essence.

4 Pour into a greased square tin and allow to stand for about 10 minutes until it begins to set.

5 Cut into squares with a sharp knife and allow to cool completely until set. Store in an air tight container.

Variations

Fruity Fudges

Cherry Fudge

Weigh out 100g/4oz glacé cherries. Chop the cherries and place them in a sieve. Pour over boiling water and pat dry with kitchen paper. Add to the fudge just before pouring into the tin.

Raisin Fudge

Heat 100g/4oz raisins in the microwave oven for 45 seconds or pop under the grill on a piece of foil for 2 minutes turning after 1 minute. Add to the fudge just before pouring in the tin.

COCONUT ICE

WHAT YOU NEED

Utensils

Bowl
Skewer
Scales
Rolling pin
Wooden spoon
Pastry board
Knife
2 sheets non-stick paper
18cm/7 in square tin

Ingredients

450g/1lb ready made moulded icing
100g/4oz desiccated coconut
1/2 teaspoon vanilla essence
Red food colouring
Makes 32 triangles

What to do

1 Mould the icing on the board until soft. Gradually work in the vanilla essence and coconut. This will take at least 5 minutes.

2 Roll the mixture into a sausage shape and cut in half.

3 Roll out one half to a square shape. Place the square in a greased 18cm/7inch square tin lined with non-stick paper.

4 Colour the remaining mixture carefully with a few drops of vegetable colouring dropped from a skewer. Work the mixture until it is an even shade of pink. Roll into a square. Place the pink mixture on top of the white and press well into the tin.

5 When the mixture is firm, cut into squares and then into triangles.

TREACLE TOFFEE

Place 450g/1lb granulated sugar in a heavy-bottomed saucepan with 150ml/$\frac{1}{4}$pint water. Allow the sugar to dissolve in the mixture, as for fudge and toffee apples, over a low heat.
When the sugar is dissolved add $\frac{1}{4}$ teaspoon cream of tartar, 75g/3oz butter, 100g/4oz golden syrup, 100g/4oz black treacle. Bring the mixture to the boil and brush the inside of the pan just above the mixture with cold water. Boil to 149°C/270°F (soft ball stage) and then pour into a 18cm/7inch shallow tin. Cool for 5 minutes then mark into squares with an oiled knife. Allow the toffee to set and remove in squares. Do not stack pieces on top of each other until dry or they will stick.

Simple Sweets

Easy-to-make sweets
for parties, presents and bazaars.

CHOCOLATE CRISPIES

WHAT YOU NEED

Utensils

Large saucepan
Knife
Wooden spoon
Tablespoon
Teaspoon
Sweet papers

Ingredients

100g/4oz dark chocolate
50g/2oz butter or
margarine
1 tablespoon golden syrup
1 tablespoon drinking
chocolate
100g/4oz rice crispies or
cornflakes
2 tablespoon sultanas
Makes 40 sweets

What to do

1 Break up the chocolate and put in the large saucepan with the butter, syrup and drinking chocolate. Stir the mixture over a gentle heat until melted and smooth.

2 Gradually add the rice crispies and stir until completely coated with chocolate.

3 Add the sultanas and mix well. Put a teaspoon of the mixture into each sweet paper.

4 Put in the fridge to set for about 2 hours.

Chocolate Crispy Cakes

This is probably the most popular recipe made in the home and is a firm favourite with all ages. To make individual crispy cakes, simply put larger spoonfuls of the chocolate mixture into cake papers and allow to set. This will give you about 15 crispy cakes. Cornflakes, branflakes or your own favourite cereal can be used. Do not use the cereals with sugar or sticky honey.

PEPPERMINT CREAMS

WHAT YOU NEED

Utensils

Skewer
Clean pastry board or
work surface
Sieve
2½cm/1 inch pastry
cutter or cocktail cutters
Baking sheet or piece of
non-stick paper

Ingredients

2 tablespoons icing sugar
250g/8oz ready made
moulded icing
Peppermint essence
Makes approx 36

What to do

1 Sift half the icing sugar on to the table or board. Mould the icing with clean hands dipped in icing sugar until it is soft and malleable.

2 Add 3-4 drops of peppermint essence into the icing and mould again to mix well.

3 Sprinkle a rolling pin with icing sugar and roll out the mixture about 1.5cm/$\frac{1}{2}$ inch thick. Cut the sweets with a round cutter and allow to dry on a tray for 24 hours lightly covered with kitchen paper.

Variation

Chocolate-coated sweets

Chocolate Peppermint Creams

When the peppermint creams have had several hours to harden, they can be half dipped into melted chocolate. Place on a sheet of non-stick paper. This gives a half chocolate half white sweet.

Chocolate Cherries

Rinse the sticky coating from 100g/4oz carton of glacé cherries. Dry with some kitchen paper. Place a cherry on to a skewer and dip into the melted chocolate. Carefully push off the skewer into a sweet paper.

Fondant Sweets

Colour the moulded icing with a few drops of green, yellow or orange food colouring and flavour with 3-4 drops vanilla or almond essence. Roll out as for peppermint creams. Press a different coloured dolly mixture into the centre of each sweet. Allow to harden and put into sweet papers.

Chocolate Truffles

Put 250g/8oz of cake crumbs into a bowl with 2 tablespoons caster sugar, 1 tablespoon cocoa powder, 2 tablespoons apricot jam, 2-3 drops rum or vanilla essence. Mix all the ingredients together with a wooden spoon. Make into small balls and roll in chocolate vermicelli which has been sprinkled on a plate. Put the truffles into sweet papers. Allow to dry for several hours before eating.

Wrappings for Sweets

If you are making sweets for presents you need to arrange them attractively.
Toffee and fudge look nice packed in cellophane squares tied with a bow of coloured ribbon. Keep sweet boxes and toffee tins from Christmas and birthdays. These can be covered with gift paper and lined with fresh tissue paper. Buy sweet papers in any large newsagents or cake shop.

Cook's Tip – Colouring and flavouring

When adding either of these to sweets use a clean metal skewer and only add a drop at a time or your sweets will be coloured bright red or have so much peppermint that the flavour is spoiled. Use a metal skewer as wooden sticks can give splinters.

Jelly Oranges

Easy to prepare and eat – have fun with oranges and jelly at parties and barbecues.

WHAT YOU NEED

Utensils

Saucepan or kettle
Measuring jug
Sharp knife
Kitchen paper
Bowl
Lemon squeezer
Grapefruit knife
Nylon sieve
Teaspoon
1 large plate

Ingredients

6 oranges
1 packet orange jelly
Serves 6

BASKETS

What to do

1 Wash the oranges and dry with kitchen paper.

2 Slice the tops from the oranges. Squeeze the juice from each orange, keep to one side. Cut around the flesh with a grapefruit knife. Remove the flesh leaving the skins whole. Rub the flesh through a nylon sieve to remove all the juice.

3 Make up the jelly with 300ml/½ pint boiling water until dissolved. Allow to cool and then stir in the orange juice making up to 600ml/1pint.

4 Arrange the orange skins on the plate, pour in the jelly and allow to set in the fridge.

5 Cut strips of orange from the tops to make 'handles' for the baskets.

Serve crispy biscuits with orange jelly baskets or slices.

ORANGE ANIMAL BISCUITS

WHAT YOU NEED

Utensils

Bowl
Sieve
Wooden spoon
Scales
Teaspoon
Rolling pin
Flour dredger
Lemon squeezer
Grater
Clingfilm

Palette knife
Pastry board
2 baking sheets
Animal cutters
Wire rack

Ingredients

50g/2oz butter or hard margarine
75g/3oz caster sugar
1 egg yolk
1 orange
2 tablespoon orange juice
150g/5oz flour
1 teaspoon baking powder
Pinch of salt
2 tablespoons caster sugar

1 Cream the butter or margarine in a bowl with the sugar until the mixture is light and fluffy. Add the egg yolk and beat well.

2 Grate the rind from half the orange and squeeze the other half for juice. Gradually add the orange rind and the juice to the mixture.

3 Sift in the flour, baking powder and salt. Mix well, shape into a roll and wrap in clingfilm. Allow to stand in the fridge for about 1 hour.

4 Pre-heat the oven to 190°C/375°F/Gas Mark 5. Roll out the dough on a floured board and cut into animal shapes. Place on a lightly greased or non-stick baking sheet. Bake in the oven for 10-12 minutes until golden brown.

5 Cool on the baking sheet for 5 minutes. Lift on to a wire cooling tray with a palette knife. Sprinkle with caster sugar while still warm.

JELLY SLICES

WHAT YOU NEED

Utensils

As for Orange Baskets

Ingredients

6 oranges
1/2 packet orange jelly
1/2 packet lime or lemon jelly
Makes 24 wedges

What to do

1 Wash the oranges and wipe dry with kitchen paper. Cut the oranges in half and scoop out the flesh with a grapefruit knife. Keep the orange flesh carefully in a dish, covered in the fridge, and use later in a fruit salad with diced apples, halved grapes and sliced bananas, raspberries or strawberries as available.

2 Make up the jellies by mixing the jelly cubes with 600ml/1pint boiling water as directed on the packets. Stand in the fridge until almost set.

3 Pour the jelly into the orange halves and allow to set in the fridge until needed.

4 Remove when firm and cut into wedges to serve.

Go Bananas

Easy to eat and prepare, bananas give you lots of energy. As a change to your usual breakfast these drinks make an ideal start to the day.

FROTHY BANANA YOGURT

WHAT YOU NEED

Utensils

Bowl
Whisk OR blender OR
food processor
fork
2 long glasses
1 tablespoon
1 sharp knife

Ingredients

300ml/¹/₂ pint skimmed
milk
2x150g/5oz cartons low
fat orange flavoured
yogurt
4 tablespoons wheatgerm
or crunchy nut cornflakes
or crumbled Weetabix
1 banana
Decoration
Slices of star fruit if liked
Makes 2-4 drinks

What to do

1 Place the milk, yogurt and 3 tablespoons cereal in a bowl or in the food processor.

2 Peel the banana and break into pieces and add to the food processor. (If using a whisk, mash the banana and add to the bowl with the other ingredients.) Whisk until fairly smooth or whizz in the food processor or blender for a few seconds until well mixed.

3 Place 2 ice cubes in each glass and pour in the orange yogurt. Decorate the top with wheatgerm or cereal. If using star fruit, arrange on the side of the glass.

BANANA STRAWBERRY SHAKE

WHAT YOU NEED

Utensils
1 sharp knife
Chopping board
1 tablespoon
1 measuring jug
Food processor or blender
2 long glasses

Ingredients

1 banana
6 large strawberries
300ml/¹/₂ pint skimmed milk
2 tablespoon icing sugar
4 tablespoons low fat yogurt
2 scoops strawberry ice-cream
(optional)
Serves 2

What to do

1 Peel the banana and break into pieces putting each piece in the food processor or blender.

2 Wash and hull the strawberries. Cut them into slices for decoration. Place the remainder into the food processor with the milk, sugar and yogurt. Add the strawberry ice-cream if using.

3 Whizz the mixture for about 45 seconds, then pour into long glasses.

4 Decorate with the strawberry slices. For special occasions slices of lime and mint leaves make pretty decorations. Serve immediately.

Fruity Punch

Just before serving add to the punch 1 eating apple, chopped into small squares,1 orange cut into rings and halved, 1 banana cut into pieces, a few sprigs of mint,3 rings of pineapple (canned or fresh) cut into small wedges and 8 strawberries cut into slices or raspberries, if available.

SPARKLING CRANBERRY CREAM

WHAT YOU NEED

Utensils

Bowl
Whisk
Fork
Large star piping nozzle
1 piping bag (optional)
2-4 sparklers (optional)
Teaspoon
2 wide-necked glasses

Ingredients

300ml/¹/₂ pint Cranberry & Raspberry Juice Drink
150ml/¹/₄ pint double cream
Decoration
8 raspberries or fresh cranberries
1 teaspoon caster sugar
Makes 2-4 glasses

What to do

1 Chill the cranberry drink in the fridge until needed.

2 Pour the cream into the bowl and whisk until thick and standing in peaks. Alternatively use cream from a can with a piping nozzle.

3 Pour the juice into the glass then pipe or fork the cream on to the top. Decorate with raspberries and cranberries which have been dredged in sugar.

4 Light the sparklers for that special party occasion. TAKE CARE! Keep sparklers well away from your face.

CRANBERRY PARTY PUNCH

WHAT YOU NEED

Utensils

Scissors
Ice tray
Large glass bowl
Ladle
8 glasses

Ingredients

2 litres/3¹/₂ pints Cranberry & Raspberry Juice Drink
2 litres/3¹/₂ pints cranberry juice
1litre/1³/₄ pint pineapple juice
1litre/1³/₄ pint grape juice
Serves 8

1 Before the party chill all the drinks for at least two hours in the refrigerator.

2 Put some ice cubes in the bottom of the bowl and pour all the ingredients in. Mix well with the ladle and serve in glasses or cups.

CHOOSING A BALANCED Diet

FOOD IS used in our bodies as fuel in much the same way as petrol makes motor cars run. The human body will use any food as fuel. But just as different engines run on different grades of fuel, the body will operate more efficiently on some foods than others. What you eat determines whether you are an unreliable banger or a finely-tuned sportscar.

It is possible to live on crisps, biscuits, cakes, chips and sugary drinks which are the favourite foods of many children, but this type of diet can lead to problems such as being overweight, having spots and low levels of concentration.

The old rule of nutrition still remains true – eat a balance of all foods everyday for a healthy body and a high energy level. This does not mean you should never drink your favourite fizzy drink or eat sweets but these foods should be limited to occasional treats. The food pyramid below helps to illustrate the proportion of foods which form a good diet.

The tip part of the pyramid shows the sugary drinks, commercially-prepared foods, sweets, sugar and fat added to food, all of which we should take in only sparingly.

A selection of high protein food like milk, yogurt, cheese, meat, fish, eggs, beans and nuts should be consumed each day in small amounts.

Lower on the pyramid is the fruit and vegetable band which provides vitamins, minerals and fibre. Try to eat lots of fresh, raw vegetables and fruit as they are better for you than cooked and especially fried vegetables.

On the bottom of the pyramid is the bread and cereal band, including pasta, rice and potatoes. These provide carbohydrates which give energy and are especially important while you are growing. These can be eaten quite freely. Beware of adding too many jams and sweet spreads to your breads. Limit cakes, sweets and fried potatoes.

Exercise is very important for a healthy life-style so join in all the games at school and with your friends – don't spend too much time sitting in front of the television. Learn to swim as this is an excellent way to exercise as well as being lots of fun. Walk briskly whenever you can and run up and down stairs.

Pyramid produced by The Flour Advisory Bureau and The Dunn Nutrition Centre

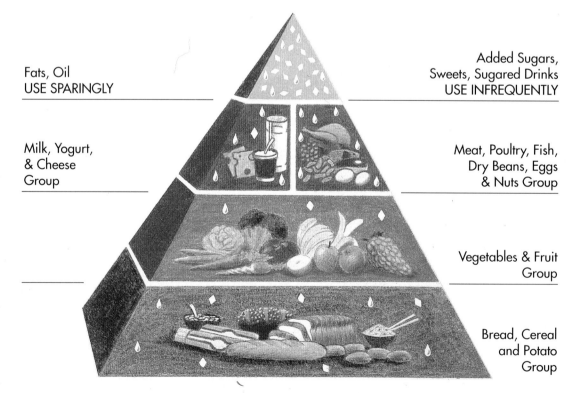

Fats, Oil
USE SPARINGLY

Added Sugars,
Sweets, Sugared Drinks
USE INFREQUENTLY

Milk, Yogurt,
& Cheese
Group

Meat, Poultry, Fish,
Dry Beans, Eggs
& Nuts Group

Vegetables & Fruit
Group

Bread, Cereal
and Potato
Group